The
Patients
Association

D1346874

a si **r**mple guide to
de pression

BESTMEDICINE Health Handbooks

A Simple Guide to Depression
First published – September 2005

Published by
CSF Medical Communications Ltd
1 Bankside, Lodge Road, Long Hanborough
Oxfordshire, OX29 8LJ, UK
T +44 (0)1993 885370 F +44 (0)1993 881868
enquiries@bestmedicine.com
www.bestmedicine.com
www.csfmedical.com

Editor Dr Eleanor Bull
Medical Editor Professor Allan Young
Creative Director & Project Manager Julia Potterton
Designer Lee Smith
Layout Julie Smith
Publisher Stephen I'Anson

contents

ACKNOWLEDGEMENTS

The *BESTMEDICINE Simple Guides* team is very grateful to a number of people who have made this project possible. In particular we'd like to thank Anne Taylor, Jane Cassidy, Caroline Delasalle and Amelie (5 months). Thank you to Ben for his endless enthusiasm, energy and creativity, to Molly (7) and George (5) and of course to Hetta. Julie and Rob who went far beyond the call of duty and Julie's ability to put pages together for hours on end was hugely inspiring.

A Simple Guide to your Health Service

Emma Catherall   Co-ordinator

Advisory Panel

Richard Stevens   GP
Spilios Argyropoulos   Psychiatrist
Michael Gum   Pharmacist
John Chater   Binley's health and care
                         information specialist
                         www.binleys.com

simple

simple *adj.* **1.** easy to understand or do: *a simple problem.* **2.** plain; unadorned: *a simple dress.* **3.** Not combined or complex: *a simple mechanism.* **4.** Unaffected or unpretentious: *although he became famous he remained a simple man.* **5.** sincere; frank: *a simple explanation was readily accepted.* **6.** (*prenominal*) without additions or modifications: *the witness told the simple truth.*

ABOUT THE AUTHOR

REBECCA FOX-SPENCER

Rebecca Fox-Spencer graduated from Cambridge University with a BA Honours degree in Natural Sciences and then completed a PhD in Neurochemistry at University College London. As well as publishing her own research work internationally, Rebecca has written for other publications in the BESTMEDICINE series. She now lives in South Oxfordshire.

ABOUT THE EDITOR

ALLAN YOUNG

Allan Young is a Professor of General Psychiatry and Director of Psychiatry at the University of Newcastle upon Tyne. He is a fellow of the Royal College of Psychiatrists and is honorary Patron of the Silver Lining Group (a depression self-help group).

FOREWORD

TRISHA MACNAIR

Doctor and BBC Health Journalist

Getting involved in managing your own medical condition – or helping those you love or care for to manage theirs – is a vital step towards keeping as healthy as possible. Whilst doctors, nurses and the rest of your healthcare team can help you with expert advice and guidance, nobody knows your body, your symptoms and what is right for *you* as well as you do.

There is no long-term (chronic) medical condition or illness that I can think of where the person concerned has absolutely no influence at all on their situation. The way you choose to live your life, from the food you eat to the exercise you take, will impact upon your disease, your well-being and how able you are to cope. You are in charge!

Being involved in making choices about your treatment helps you to feel in control of your problems, and makes sure you get the help that you really need. Research clearly shows that when people living with a chronic illness take an active role in looking after themselves, they can bring about significant improvements in their illness and vastly improve the quality of life they enjoy. Of course, there may be occasions when you feel particularly unwell and it all seems out of your control. Yet most of the time there are plenty of things that you can do in order to reduce the negative effects that your condition can have on your life. This way you feel as good as possible and may even be able to alter the course of your condition.

So how do you gain the confidence and skills to take an active part in managing your condition, communicate with health professionals and work through sometimes worrying and emotive issues? The answer is to become better informed. Reading about your problem, talking to others who have been through similar experiences and hearing what the experts have to say will all help to build-up your understanding and help you to take an active role in your own health care.

BESTMEDICINE Simple Guides provide an invaluable source of help, giving you the facts that you need in order to understand the key issues and discuss them with your doctors and other professionals involved in your care. The information is presented in an accessible way but without neglecting the important details. Produced independently and under the guidance of medical experts *A Simple Guide to Depression* is an evidence-based, balanced and up-to-date review that I hope you will find enables you to play an active part in the successful management of your condition.

what happens normally?

WHAT HAPPENS NORMALLY?

We may often feel sad or depressed, but we are not all ill. How do we know what's normal, and what's not?

Life is full of ups and downs. As well as the good things in life, we all experience stress, failure, disagreements, exclusion and even bereavement. It is only natural that we let things get to us from time-to-time. In extreme cases, some experiences completely knock us for six – an unexpected death of a loved one, for example – and it can feel like we have hit an absolute low.

But we bounce back. Each in our own individual way, we deal with the problems that life throws at us, and sooner or later, we are back on our feet.

A healthy person can deal with even the most harrowing experiences whilst keeping things in perspective. Sure, for a while it might seem like nothing can ever be the same again, like it's not worth making an effort… but these feelings subside pretty quickly, and they do not colour every aspect of life. A healthy individual can appreciate that there is a light at the end of the tunnel, and even if they seem to be in a constant bad mood, they can appreciate that they will feel better, given time.

The emotional brain

Whether we feel low or elated, our emotions all stem from patterns of activity in our brains. It would be a vast over-simplification to say that you have a 'mood centre' in your brain, and your state of happiness depends on how busy this centre is. On the other hand, there *are* distinct regions and structures in the brain that scientists have identified as playing some role in how we feel.

fMRI highlights areas of activity in the brain by detecting increased blood flow in these regions.

Much of our understanding about the roles of these brain regions has arisen from the use of scanning techniques by scientists. Using methods such as **fMRI** (functional magnetic resonance imaging) scientists are able to detect which regions of the brain are most active when a person is performing different mental or physical tasks.

You don't need to know exactly how the brain controls your emotions – even the world's top neuroscientists don't fully understand this! In order to get a better idea of what goes wrong in depression, though, it will be useful for you to recognise a few of the more important parts of the brain when it comes to controlling your mood and behaviour.

Emotional centres in the brain

The term 'amygdala' is derived from the Greek word for 'almond'. The amygdala is 'almond-like' in both its shape and size.

■ **Amygdala** involved in:
– generating emotions such as fear
– prioritising thoughts and keeping things in context.
■ **Hippocampus** involved in:
– forming memories
– keeping emotional responses in context and ensuring that your reactions are appropriate.
■ **Prefrontal cortex** involved in:
– determining complex aspects of your personality, especially 'reward-seeking behaviour'
– problem solving.
■ **Cingulate cortex** involved in:
– connecting the regions of your brain that are involved in emotions and attention
– decision making
– ability to feel pleasure.

When your mood or behaviour changes, these regions of the brain become more or less busy, which can be shown using fMRI scans. Changes in activity in the brain are happening all the time – they are an essential part of how the brain works.

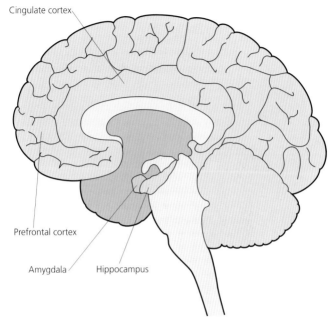

Cingulate cortex

Prefrontal cortex

Amygdala   Hippocampus

THE EMOTIONAL CENTRES IN THE BRAIN.

However, if feelings of low mood persist for any reason, such as during the baby blues or a period of grief, more persistent changes can occur. These involve depletion in the levels of chemicals, called **neurotransmitters**, which are needed in order for brain cells to communicate with each other properly. However, these changes are temporary, and normal neurotransmitter levels and brain activity are restored when the mood improves.

Approximately half of new mothers in the UK experience the 'baby blues', which normally set in a few days after child birth. The baby blues go away on their own, and are considered 'normal'.

When it stops being normal

Sometimes, the normal period of low mood that follows a difficult experience, such as the break-up of a relationship or losing your job, can persist beyond a few weeks and become more sinister. On the other hand, there may be no clear trigger for some very negative feelings, which nonetheless won't go away and begin to affect other aspects of life. Changes can occur in the brain that are more permanent than just a lull in brain activity or a temporary depletion of neurotransmitter chemicals.

When it occurs, 'clinical depression' is a very different kettle of fish to the low moods that we all feel from time-to-time.

the basics

DEPRESSION – THE BASICS

Determining what is a normal fluctuation in mood and what constitutes true depression can be very difficult, but depression is a highly treatable disease.

The problem with the term 'depressed' is that people use it every day to describe a general feeling of sadness or being fed up. The challenge for you, and indeed your doctor, is to identify at what point depression ceases being 'normal' and becomes an illness which needs treating.

Regardless of whether or not you have experienced a distressing event which you might expect to trigger a period of low mood, you may have true depression if:

■ your negative feelings persist for more than 2 weeks

■ the feelings are severe enough to interfere with your work, relationships and everyday life.

Generally, when people refer to depression in a medical sense, they mean 'clinical depression', which can be classified as mild, as well as moderate or severe. In its most serious form, severe depression is accompanied by psychotic symptoms, such as hallucinations or delusions. On the other hand, mild depression which lasts for over 2 years is known medically as **dysthymia**.

As well as clinical depression *per se*, there are other types of depression recognised by doctors in the UK:

- **seasonal affective disorder** – 'winter depression'.
- **postnatal depression** – more persistent and more serious than the 'baby blues'.

Also, when episodes of depression are interspersed with periods of mental and physical hyperactivity, or 'mania', this is known as **bipolar disorder** (previously and more commonly referred to as manic depression).

Bipolar disorder will not be covered further in this book, but will be the subject of a future title within the *Simple Guide* series.

Clinical depression		
Mild		
Moderate		
Severe	No psychotic symptoms	
	Psychotic symptoms	

Dysthymia (long-term, mild depression)	Post-natal depression	Seasonal affective disorder	Bipolar disorder 'manic depression'

THE DIFFERENT TYPES OF DEPRESSION.

SYMPTOMS

As you would expect, there are a wide range of psychological symptoms associated with clinical depression, in that they affect your mood and behaviour, and your general way of thinking. You may not have realised, however, that depression can also have physical symptoms – aches and pains, which have no immediately obvious cause. These can act as a bit of a 'red herring' for you, and indeed your doctor, in identifying that depression is the underlying problem.

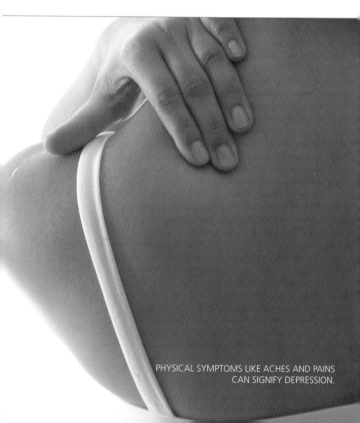

PHYSICAL SYMPTOMS LIKE ACHES AND PAINS CAN SIGNIFY DEPRESSION.

If you have clinical depression, you may be familiar with some of these typical symptoms:

- preoccupation with negative thoughts, particularly in the morning
- having a bleak view of the future
- being restless and irritable
- sleeping badly, often with excessive dreaming
- exhaustion
- abnormal eating, leading to weight loss or gain
- feeling very emotional and crying often
- difficulty concentrating, making decisions and remembering things
- poor motivation
- loss of interest in activities you used to enjoy
- feelings of guilt and worthlessness
- anxiety (emotional and physical symptoms in anticipation of real or imagined danger)
- helplessness and desperation
- low expectations of improvements in your mood (no 'light at the end of the tunnel')
- physical aches and pains without apparent cause
- self-harm, suicidal thoughts or actions.

Depression was described in the Bible – King David, King Saul and Job were all reported to have depressive symptoms.

CAUSES OF DEPRESSION

Why do you have depression? There are a number of factors which are thought to cause or worsen depression, and these can generally be divided into two groups – biological factors and environmental factors.

Biological factors:

- inheritance of an increased risk from your parents
- depleted levels of neurotransmitters in your brain.

Environmental factors:

- traumatic life experiences
- learning negative ways of thinking via interactions with parents/teachers/peers
- drug or alcohol abuse
- hormonal changes.

DIAGNOSING DEPRESSION

As there is no simple blood test or scan for clinical depression its diagnosis can be extremely challenging. In diagnosing depression, your GP will take account of your:

■ symptoms
■ recent and past medical history
■ family history
■ physical condition
■ personal history (i.e. relationships, education, employment, social activities).

There are a number of possible reasons for your persistent low mood other than depression itself. Your doctor will need to check whether these apply in your case before deciding how best to manage your symptoms. Alternative causes include:

■ other medical conditions
■ side-effects from drugs used to treat other medical conditions
■ abuse of drugs or alcohol.

Your doctor will probably also want to know whether you have recently lost a friend or loved one, as bereavement can affect some people for quite a long time. It is important to distinguish normal bereavement from depression which requires treatment.

MANAGING DEPRESSION

There are a number of strategies which your doctor can use to manage your depression.

'Watchful waiting'

This is a period during which your doctor will monitor you closely without giving you any other treatment. This is an important part of the management procedure, as it is not in your best interests to receive treatments for depression if your condition is not severe enough to warrant their use.

'Talking treatments'

These treatments target the psychological component of depression. They aim to teach you how to think more positively, and help you to deal with problems with work and relationships, for example, in a more constructive way. The most common talking treatments are:

- counselling
- cognitive behavioural therapy (CBT)
- problem-solving therapy
- interpersonal psychotherapy (including couple-focused therapy)
- guided self-help
- befriending.

Antidepressant drugs

Antidepressants target the biological component of depression. They help to increase the activity of chemicals called neurotransmitters in the brain. This allows the different regions of the brain involved in controlling your emotions to function properly again. The numerous drugs available can be grouped into four main classes:

■ tricyclic antidepressants (TCAs)
■ monoamine oxidase inhibitors (MAOIs)
■ selective serotonin reuptake inhibitors (SSRIs)
■ atypical antidepressants.

Other treatments

There are a number of alternative or complementary treatments for depression, which include:

■ St John's wort
■ electroconvulsive therapy (ECT)
■ exercise
■ acupuncture
■ herbal medicine
■ meditation
■ yoga.

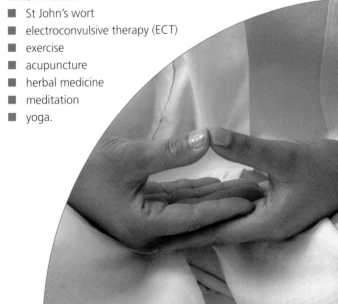

More than 80% of patients with depression are treated at their GP practice without being referred to a specialist.

There is a good chance that you will not need to be referred to a specialist for treatment of your depression. This does not mean, though, that your GP will be the only one helping you to get better. The responsibility of your care starts with you, your family and friends and your GP, and may also involve the following professionals:

- mental health nurse
- community psychiatric nurse
- counsellor
- social worker
- practice nurse
- psychiatrist
- clinical psychologist
- occupational therapist
- pharmacist
- fitness trainer.

If your depression is very severe, you may be admitted to hospital, where you will be looked after by specialists.

The most important step in overcoming your depression is to recognise that depressive symptoms are more extreme than the normal fluctuations in mood that everyone experiences from day-to-day, and that you need to seek help. Once it has been diagnosed, depression is a treatable condition. Please don't struggle on alone.

why me?

WHY ME?

People with depression often feel ashamed, embarrassed and unsure of why they have the condition. It may help you to know how common depression actually is, and to understand what might have caused it in your case.

WHO GETS DEPRESSION?

For a person who is depressed, isolation is often one of the overriding feelings. If you feel this way, it may help you to know that depression is far more common than people often realise.

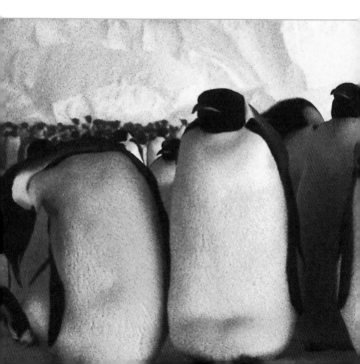

- Depression is the most common mental disorder in the world, thought to affect around 120 million people.
- At some point in their lives, roughly 1 in 5 women in the UK and 1 in 10 men, experience depression which is serious enough to warrant treatment.
- Approximately 1 in 7 elderly people (over the age of 65) experience symptoms of depression, though it is under-recognised and under-treated in people from this age group.
- Although rare in children under the age of 8, roughly 3% of all children experience depression. It is more common in adolescents (approximately 4–8%), particularly amongst girls.

In 2000, depression was the fourth most important contributor to the global burden of disease.

If you look at the worldwide prevalence of depression (the percentage of the population with depression) on the map below, you will notice that there is no clear pattern of depression in the developed world compared with the developing world. Different factors might cause depression in different kinds of society:

■ poverty and poor levels of sanitation might cause depression in developing countries

■ high levels of stress and expectations might cause depression in developed countries.

It is interesting to note that, of all the countries shown in the map, the UK has the second highest rate of depression.

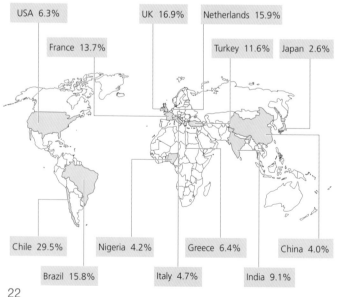

USA 6.3%

UK 16.9%

Netherlands 15.9%

France 13.7%

Turkey 11.6%

Japan 2.6%

Chile 29.5%

Nigeria 4.2%

Greece 6.4%

China 4.0%

Brazil 15.8%

Italy 4.7%

India 9.1%

WHY DO I HAVE DEPRESSION?

In many cases, depression is triggered by an unpleasant life experience, such as:

■ the death of a friend or relative
■ losing a job
■ the break-up of a relationship or a divorce
■ failure in an exam, test or interview
■ chronic illness (e.g. arthritis) or infections (e.g. influenza)
■ moving away from home.

You may hear this kind of depression referred to as **reactive depression**. On the other hand, depression which is not obviously associated with any particular event has been labelled **endogenous depression**. However, these terms are not used very often anymore as there does not appear to be any difference in the way that they affect the brain or in the symptoms they cause.

Depression may also occur as a direct side-effect of drugs which you may be taking for other medical reasons, such as:

■ drugs used for lowering blood pressure
■ the oral contraceptive pill
■ steroid drugs used for managing inflammatory conditions like rheumatoid arthritis.

The use or abuse of recreational drugs or alcohol can also bring on depression.

Regardless of whether or not your depression is triggered by an obvious cause, there are two main factors which will affect your risk of becoming depressed:

■ your family history
■ your life experiences.

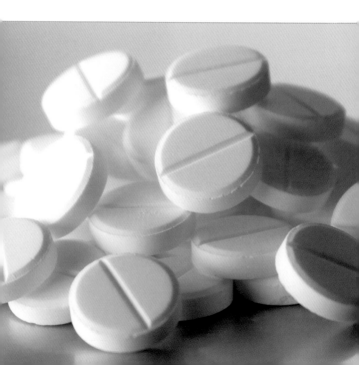

Family history

You cannot inherit depression, as such. There is no evidence of a single gene that can be passed on to you by your parents, which will make it inevitable that you will develop depression, as is the case for a disease like cystic fibrosis. However, if your immediate family has a history of depression or another mental illness, you can inherit a certain vulnerability to developing depression.

It is important to remember that children learn behaviour from their parents and siblings. If a parent is depressed, and approaches situations with a negative attitude, their children will probably learn to deal with things in a similar way. Scientists have investigated this by looking at adopted children, and have found that these children are more likely to develop depression if their biological parent showed signs of mental illness, regardless of the mental state of their adoptive parents, with whom they grow up. Therefore, whilst learned behaviour is probably an important factor in the risk of developing depression, you can also inherit an increased susceptibility to depression in your genes.

There is some genetic component to depression, but inheriting this risk is not enough on its own to cause it.

25

Life experiences

Regardless of whether or not you experience a specific event that triggers depression, the accumulation of events that happen to you during your lifetime are critical in determining the likelihood of you developing depression. As well as the trigger events we have already considered, experiences which may contribute to you developing depression include:

- living in a violent household
- loss or trauma in early life (e.g. birth trauma in the newborn, abuse, neglect, loss of a parent [through death or divorce])
- extreme stress
- poor social conditions (e.g. poverty, homelessness)
- failures (at work or socially) which undermine your self-confidence
- hormonal changes (e.g. menopause) childbirth
- lifestyle (e.g. lack of exercise, being over/underweight).

Learned helplessness

Another factor which can make you more susceptible to developing depression in later life is the concept of 'learned helplessness'. Possibly the easiest way to understand this is to consider some experiments that have been performed on rats. These experiments were done some time ago, back in the 1960s, and were not particularly pleasant. Looking at the findings of these experiments, however, gives a useful illustration of how the way that you are treated by others can affect your behaviour.

Imagine two groups of rats. All of the rats are trained to expect that when they hear a buzzer, a few seconds later they will experience a small (unpleasant, but not physically damaging) shock. The first group of rats can avoid the shock by moving to a safe area, but for the second group, the shock is unavoidable.

Following their training, all of the rats are then put into a tank of water (don't worry – rats are good swimmers!). Whereas the rats from the first group happily swim to the edge, the second group give up very quickly and need rescuing, even though they are physically capable. Their earlier experience has taught them that they cannot avoid bad things happening however hard they try. This is '**learned helplessness**'.

These observations translate to human behaviour. In cases where a person has been subjected to pain or distress which they could not avoid through any action of their own, they are then much more likely to admit defeat in the future, which is a big part of being depressed. Examples of these 'no way out' situations include imprisonment, rape and childhood abuse. They need not, however, be so extreme – a similar effect can result from a child being continually put down by a teacher.

EXTREME SITUATIONS SUCH AS IMPRISONMENT CAN LEAD TO DEPRESSION.

Other factors

Age

Since 1940, the average age of the first experience of depression has fallen from the mid 30s to the late 20s.

It is often assumed that your risk of becoming depressed increases with your age, but this is not true – the most common age to first experience depression is your late 20s.

Gender

You are more likely to experience depression if you are female – about twice as likely, in fact. Several of the life experiences which contribute to the risk of depression are specific to, or at least more common in, women. These include hormonal changes, childbirth and stress due to balancing a job and motherhood, for example.

Although depression is less common in men than women, men are three times more likely than women to commit suicide.

Depression is often harder to spot in men as they have a tendency to mask it with alcohol, by working longer hours and by appearing irritable, angry and discouraged. Men are also less likely to ask for help and so the higher risk in women may be biased somewhat by the fact that many more men remain undiagnosed. It may also account for the higher suicide rate in men, who have a tendency to allow their depression to reach a more serious stage before seeking help.

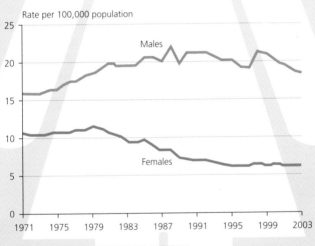

Rate per 100,000 population

Males

Females

1971   1975   1979   1983   1987   1991   1995   1999   2003

SUICIDE RATES IN MEN AND WOMEN IN THE UK.

ETHNICITY

There does not appear to be any clear link between race and depression. Your race is unlikely to have contributed to you becoming depressed, unless it has made you the subject of racist attitudes, which may have had a social impact on your confidence.

Social status

Given that living in poverty or being homeless are life experiences which contribute to the risk of depression, it is hardly surprising that depression is more common amongst people with a low social status. However, this is not to say that people who are well-off do not get depressed. You only need to consider the numerous celebrities who have reported suffering from depression to see that a substantial income and a glamorous lifestyle do not prevent it! The stress that is associated with having a high profile or a lot of responsibility can outweigh the added security that money provides.

Creativity

A less clear-cut risk factor for depression is your creativity. People who are particularly creative, such as artists, actors, and perhaps scientists and other academics, are more likely to suffer mental disorders such as depression. Examples of famous creative thinkers to have suffered from depression include Wolfgang Amadeus Mozart, Victor Hugo, Mark Twain and Ernest Hemingway. This may be because creative people:

- receive little encouragement, praise or payment for much of their work
- are more likely to work alone, and spend more time dwelling on problems
- may come under fire for unusual or controversial opinions
- are less likely to agree to treatment in case it interferes with the way they express themselves.

LANDMARKS IN THE HISTORY OF DEPRESSION

Fifth century BC

Depression was recognised in ancient Greece in the Hippocratic writings (by the name 'melancholia', meaning 'black bile'). Hippocrates taught that thoughts and feelings originated in the brain, rather than the heart, as was believed at the time.

Second century BC

A Roman, Cicero, rejected Hippocrates' suggestion that melancholia was caused by 'black bile', and claimed it was due to violent rage, fear and grief.

First century

A Roman medical philosopher, Arateus, identified that manic and depressive states could occur in the same person (the foundations of bipolar disorder).

Fourteenth and fifteenth century

People with mental health problems were considered to be witches, and were persecuted.

Seventeenth to nineteenth century

European spa towns, such as Bath, gained popularity as people 'took the waters' for their nervous complaints. Melancholia was described as a 'particularly English' condition!

1812

The American physician Benjamin Rush claimed that 'the cause of madness is seated primarily in the blood vessels of the brain'.

1823

A German professor, Johann Christian Heinroth, identified factors such as food, drink, sleep, exercise and air pollution as affecting mental well-being.

Nineteenth century

Sigmund Freud championed hypnosis for neuroses and depression, due to its ability to reveal buried childhood memories.

Early twentieth century
Barbiturates were used to render depressed patients unconscious for several days, with the theory that they would have a healthier frame of mind on awakening.

1928
The Austrian scientist Otto Loewi discovered the first neurotransmitter – acetylcholine.

1938
A controlled fit, induced by electricity, was first used as a treatment for depression. This followed the observation that people with epilepsy have less severe symptoms of mental illness.

1958
Swiss scientists identified that a new antituberculosis drug made schizophrenic patients more agitated. It also turned out to make depressed patients more sociable, interested in life, and gave them an increased appetite. The drug was imipramine, and is still used to treat depression today.

1950s and 1960s
It was identified that some drugs with antidepressant properties affected serotonin levels, and in particular, prevented its reuptake into neurons.

1960s onwards
The popularity of 'talking treatments' increased.

1980s
Forty different neurotransmitters had been isolated by this time.

1987
The first selective serotonin reuptake inhibitor was launched – fluoxetine (Prozac®).

1994
Fluoxetine (Prozac®) became the second best selling drug in the world.

2004
Venlafaxine (Efexor®) was the top selling antidepressant, and the tenth best selling drug in the world.

WHEN DEPRESSION TAKES CONTROL

A major concern associated with depression is the risk of self-harm or even suicide. The risk of suicide in people with severe depression is over four times higher than that amongst the non-depressed population.

Mental illness and the risk of suicide featured heavily in a proposal set out by the government in 1999 aimed at improving the health of the UK population. This White Paper, entitled *Saving Lives: Our Healthier Nation* specifically highlighted the government's aim to "reduce the death rate from suicide and undetermined injury by at least one-fifth by 2010 – saving up to 4,000 lives in total."

If you ever have thoughts about suicide, you must tell your doctor as soon as possible. If you feel in immediate danger of self-harm, get emergency help straight away.

Depression is an unpleasant condition. It is important for you to try to regain control of your life, and make a conscious decision not to let it beat you. Feeling in control is an important step forward in overcoming your depression.

simple science

SIMPLE SCIENCE

There is a good chance that you will be prescribed antidepressant drugs as part of your treatment. In order to understand how these drugs work, you need to understand a little bit about the chemical changes that may have occurred in your brain.

As we have already seen, everyday changes in the mood of a healthy person can be accompanied by changes in the levels of chemicals in the brain. These chemicals are collectively called **neurotransmitters**, and some of them affect our mood, feelings and personality. Let's first take a look at what neurotransmitters are for, and then we will see how a simple chemical can control something as complex as our emotions.

BRIDGING THE GAPS

Cells are the individual units that make up all tissues in the body, like the brain, liver, heart and muscles. All living organisms are made up of at least one cell.

Your brain is full of billions of cells, or **neurons**. The way that your brain works depends on these neurons communicating with each other, by means of electrical signals. The neurons form complex networks in your brain, and the electrical signals speed around these networks, being passed from one neuron to the next. Think of these signals as being a bit like passengers moving around a horribly complicated (but incredibly efficient!) railway network – the train lines represent the neurons.

Synapses

Within these networks, neurons are not physically connected to one another. There are small gaps between them which interrupt the path of the electrical signal. These gaps are called **synaptic clefts**. The combination of the end of one neuron (the so-called pre-synaptic neuron), the point where it nearly meets a second cell (the post-synaptic neuron), and the synaptic cleft between them is known as a **synapse**. In our rail network analogy, think of the synapses as stations, at which passengers can get off one train line in order to continue their journey on another one.

It is inside the pre-synaptic neuron that neurotransmitters are stored, within little packages known as vesicles.

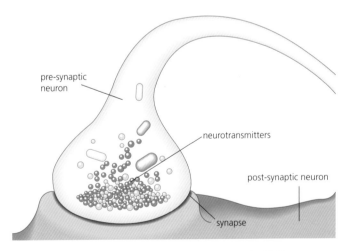

SYNAPSES ARE THE JUNCTIONS BETWEEN NERVE CELLS OR NEURONS.

Communicating across synapses

In order for the two neurons to communicate, the electrical signal needs to jump across the synapse. This is where the neurotransmitter comes in.

1 The electrical signal arrives at the end of the pre-synaptic neuron.

2 This triggers the neurotransmitter chemical to be released from the inside of this first neuron into the synaptic cleft.

3 The neurotransmitter moves across the cleft, and lands on the surface of the post-synaptic neuron.

4 Tiny receptors on this surface act as 'start buttons' for the second cell. When the neurotransmitter arrives on these receptors, an electrical signal is triggered in the second cell, and the signal continues its journey on to the next synapse.

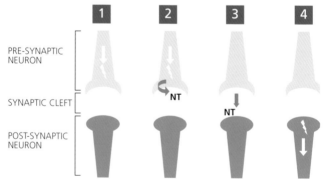

PRE-SYNAPTIC NEURON

SYNAPTIC CLEFT

POST-SYNAPTIC NEURON

NT – neurotransmitter

Transmission across a synapse is the slowest part of the journey of an electrical nerve impulse. However, synaptic clefts are pretty tiny – you could fit 20,000 of them into 1 mm. Altogether, these four steps take about five-thousandths of a second!

You may wonder why we need synapses. Why not simply have long neurons which carry each signal directly to its destination? It is because neurons do not simply have one synapse at their beginning and one at their end – they have many more. Think of the train lines – there is not a single, uninterrupted line for every single journey a passenger could possibly wish to take – that would be ridiculous! Instead, stations provide the opportunity to switch lines, so that any journey is possible whilst keeping the number of individual lines to a minimum. The same reasoning applies in the brain.

The strength of the electrical signal

The successful transmission of the signal from one neuron to the next depends on:

- enough neurotransmitter being released into the synaptic cleft
- the neurotransmitter remaining in the synaptic cleft for a sufficient duration of time.

Not all electrical signals travelling around networks of neurons are the same strength. The amount of neurotransmitter released from the pre-synaptic neuron determines how strong the electrical signal will be in the post-synaptic neuron. In a healthy person, there is more than enough neurotransmitter stored at the ends of pre-synaptic neurons to be able to convey any strength of signal across the synapses.

Removing the neurotransmitter

Once the neurotransmitter has done its job, it needs to be removed from the synaptic cleft to prevent it from repeatedly and inappropriately triggering the electrical impulse in the post-synaptic neuron. It is taken back into the pre-synaptic neuron by a process aptly called **reuptake**. There, it will either be taken back into the vesicles and stored, so it can be used again, or broken down. The breakdown, and therefore inactivation, of these neurotransmitters is carried out by an enzyme called **monoamine oxidase**.

An enzyme is a naturally occurring protein which speeds up specific chemical reactions in the body.

THE CHEMICAL MESSENGERS IN DEPRESSION

There are many different types of neurotransmitter in the brain, but two are particularly relevant when we're thinking about emotions and depression. They are:

■ serotonin
■ noradrenaline.

A third neurotransmitter, dopamine, also appears to play some role in depression.

Dopamine is another neurotransmitter, also involved in controlling emotions and behaviour, though it probably has a smaller role than serotonin or noradrenaline.

THE EMOTIONAL BRAIN

There are certain regions of the brain which are particularly involved in your emotions, behaviour and personality:

- the amygdala
- the hippocampus
- the prefrontal cortex
- the cingulate cortex.

Although the relationship between neurotransmitters and depression is by no means clear-cut, the brains of people who are depressed tend to demonstrate lower levels of activity of the neurotransmitters serotonin and noradrenaline. Each neuron in the brain tends to use one main kind of neurotransmitter. Scientists have begun to establish in which parts of the brain these two neurotransmitters are used, and as you can see, there is considerable overlap with the emotional regions described above.

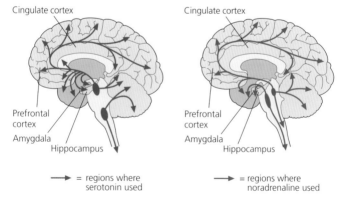

THE PATHWAYS USING SEROTONIN AND NORADRENALINE IN THE BRAIN.

In other words, if either or both of serotonin and noradrenaline are lacking in the brain, this will put a restriction on how active the emotional areas can be, because the electrical signals will be stalled at the synapses. This restricted activity is the best understood 'biological basis' of depression.

There is an important long-term implication of this reduced activity. An interesting feature of neurons is that they need to stay active in order to maintain their structure and function. If a region of your brain is underactive for any considerable length of time, it will actually start to shrink as redundant neurons are killed off.

As you will see later, antidepressant drugs work by increasing the amount of, or mimicking, serotonin and noradrenaline, in order to allow neurons in the emotional regions of the brain to communicate with each other more effectively. This allows the emotional regions of the brain to remain more active.

THE CHICKEN AND THE EGG IN DEPRESSION

Scientists think that the function of neurotransmitters is impaired in people who have depression. As a result, it has been suggested that a lack of neurotransmitter activity *causes* depression. This was the driving force behind developing drugs which increased the levels of these neurotransmitters or mimicked their actions.

However, antidepressant drugs – even the most recently developed ones – are only effective in between two-thirds and three-quarters of people with depression. As these drugs do not work in 100% of cases, experts now believe that it is not a simple case of low levels of chemicals in the brain being the cause, and depression the outcome.

We know that the activity of neurotransmitters in the brain affects your behaviour and your way of thinking. However, your behaviour and way of thinking also affect the activity of neurotransmitters in the brain. You can see, therefore, that depression involves a vicious circle of behaviour and brain chemistry.

What is not really clear is at what point this downward spiral begins – it is a bit of a chicken and egg situation. Although reduced levels of neurotransmitter activity appear to be involved in the development of depression, they may not have been the source of the problem. If something else triggered the low mood in the first place – such as having a family history of depression or various life experiences – treating the chemical changes is only addressing part of the problem.

This probably explains why antidepressant drugs are not effective in all patients. In particular, antidepressants are less effective in people whose depression was triggered by a stressful event. It also makes sense of the fact that these drugs generally work best when used in combination with 'talking treatments', which are aimed at changing thinking patterns and addressing possible lifestyle causes of depression.

HOW DO ANTIDEPRESSANT DRUGS WORK?

Antidepressants are designed to increase the effects of the two neurotransmitters primarily involved in depression – serotonin and noradrenaline. Antidepressant drugs are grouped into a number of classes, according to the way they affect the serotonin and noradrenaline systems.

Tricyclic antidepressants (TCAs)

TCAs improve transmission of the electrical impulse across the synapse by blocking the reuptake of both serotonin and noradrenaline into pre-synaptic nerves. This means that serotonin and noradrenaline remain in synaptic clefts for longer, increasing the strength of the signals passed on to post-synaptic neurons. In other words TCAs maintain the connections for longer.

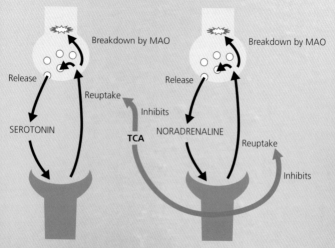

TCAs: MECHANISM OF ACTION.

Examples of TCAs include amitriptyline hydrochloride (Triptafen®, Triptafen-M®) and doxepin (Sinequan®).

Monoamine oxidase inhibitors (MAOIs)

During treatment with MAOIs, serotonin and noradrenaline are taken back up into pre-synaptic neurons as normal after they have been used to transmit a signal across a synapse. However, MAOIs inhibit the enzyme monoamine oxidase (MAO), which is responsible for breaking the neurotransmitters down and therefore inactivating them. By reducing this inactivation process, these drugs increase the amount of serotonin and noradrenaline available for when they are next needed. In other words, MAOIs help to establish a reservoir of chemical messengers. Examples of MAOIs include phenelzine (Nardil®), isocarboxazid and moclobemide (Manerix®).

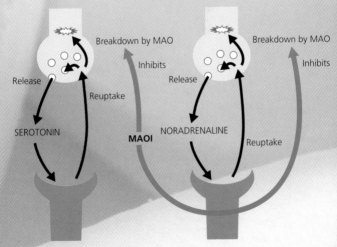

MAOIs: MECHANISM OF ACTION.

Selective serotonin reuptake inhibitors (SSRIs)

These drugs increase the level of serotonin in the synaptic cleft by blocking its reuptake into the pre-synaptic neuron. Similarly to TCAs, therefore, they increase the strength of the signal passed onto the post-synaptic neuron by keeping the neurotransmitter in the synaptic cleft for longer. They are selective for serotonin, however, and do not have any significant effects on the noradrenaline system. Like TCAs, SSRIs help maintain the connection for longer. Examples of SSRIs include citalopram (Cipramil®), fluoxetine (Prozac®) and paroxetine (Seroxat®).

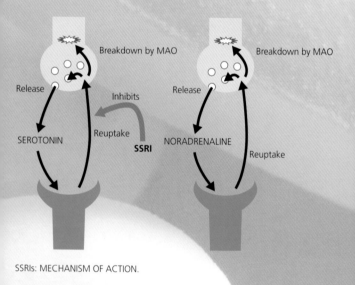

SSRIs: MECHANISM OF ACTION.

Atypical antidepressants

Antidepressant drugs which do not fit into the other three classes are called atypical antidepressants.

- *Venlafaxine (Efexor®, Efexor® XL)* – inhibits the reuptake of serotonin, noradrenaline, and to a certain extent, dopamine.
- *Flupentixol (Fluanxol®)* – thought to increase the amount of dopamine released from pre-synaptic neurons.
- *Mirtazapine (Zispin SolTab®)* – increases the amount of serotonin and noradrenaline released from pre-synaptic neurons.
- *Reboxetine (Edronax®)* – inhibits the reuptake of noradrenaline into the pre-synaptic neuron.
- *Tryptophan (Optimax®)* – increases serotonin levels. An unpleasant side-effect known as eosinophilia-myalgia syndrome led to controls on tryptophan in the UK which have now been lifted.
- *Maprotilene (Ludiomil®), mianserin (Mianserin) and trazodone (Molipaxin®)* – related to TCAs, but have slightly different properties, and vary in the extent of their effects on the serotonin and noradrenaline systems.

Tryptophan is actually found in foods that we eat. In the body, it is used to make serotonin.

HORMONES AND DEPRESSION

It is not only chemicals in the brain that affect your mood and behaviour. It is likely that **hormones** also play a role in the development of depression, and this may offer an explanation as to why depression is so closely linked with feelings of stress.

When something in your environment makes you stressed – let's say you are confronted by a snarling guard dog – your hormones react in a way that prepares your body to deal with the situation:

A hormone is a naturally occurring chemical which is made by specialised cells and released into the bloodstream.

- A part of your brain called the **hypothalamus** releases a hormone called **corticotropin-releasing factor (CRF)**.
- CRF travels to a second brain region called the **pituitary gland**, and triggers it to release another hormone, **adrenocorticotropic hormone (ACTH)**.
- ACTH travels in the blood down to two small glands perched on top of the kidneys (called the **adrenal glands**) and triggers them to release a third hormone, called **cortisol**.

These three hormones, CRF, ACTH and cortisol, work together to prepare your body to deal with the source of the stress – the guard dog. They make you alert, increase your heart rate and blood pressure, prime your muscles for action, and can also make

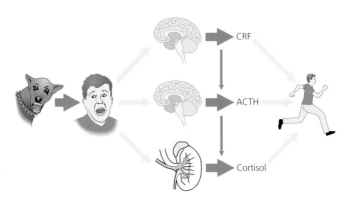

HOW HORMONES HELP YOU REACT TO STRESSFUL SITUATIONS.

you feel scared and anxious. The same hormone response occurs when the stress you experience is emotional (such as a heated argument with a loved one).

In a healthy person, the levels of these hormones return to normal once the stressful situation is over. In people who are depressed, however, the stress hormone system is overactive. Persistent feelings of stress are a recognised trigger for depression, and depressed people tend to have abnormally high levels of cortisol in their blood, even in the absence of an obvious stressful event. Not only that, but scientists have shown that injecting CRF into animals makes them act as if they are depressed.

A promising way of treating depression in the future is, therefore, to try and bring the activity of the stress hormone system back down to normal levels. To this end, scientists are attempting to develop drugs which will counteract the effects of CRF or block the effects of increased levels of cortisol.

managing
depression

MANAGING DEPRESSION

The most difficult step in managing depression properly is achieving a diagnosis. If you are diagnosed with depression, a team of healthcare professionals will help you to control your condition and find long-term solutions which will prevent it from coming back.

WHAT WILL HAPPEN TO ME?

If it is not treated properly, depression rears its head again within 2 years in nearly 90% of patients.

Clinical depression is a chronic condition, and there is no quick fix. If it is left untreated, an episode of depression lasts, on average, around 9 months. Do not be encouraged to let it run its natural course though – the problem with leaving depression to sort itself out is that it is very likely to come back.

You will need to be patient when it comes to managing your depression. Most treatment options take some weeks to start working, and no treatment is guaranteed to be effective. Your doctor will work with you to develop the management strategy most suitable for you. It is important to always feel that you are in control of your life and your depression, rather than vice versa. A sense of self-control is very useful for combating depression.

Your family can be an important source of support throughout your treatment. Try not to feel guilty about being a burden – remember that exaggerated feelings of guilt are a symptom of depression. Your family

FIVE WAYS TO HELP YOURSELF

1 Keep in close contact with your friends.

2 Get plenty of exercise.

3 Have a healthy, balanced diet.

4 Take control of your life – set small and realistic goals.

5 Consult your doctor regularly.

would probably rather that you were upfront about your condition. Do remember, though, that it may be distressing for them to see you like this, and you should not rely entirely on the support of your family. Make sure you have professional medical care as well.

Seek help and support from close friends as well as your family. Your friends may be able to offer a fresh approach.

DIAGNOSIS

More than half of all people with depression in the UK do not visit their GP to ask for help.

The most nerve-wracking and difficult part of the whole depression management process can be plucking up the courage to go to your GP in the first place. You may not be sure that you have depression, and not want to waste their time. However, if you can relate to the symptoms described in this book, don't be afraid to do so. Remember that even mild depression often needs some kind of treatment, so let your doctor be the judge of how to manage your condition – they are the experts!

Guidelines for diagnosis

There are a number of guidelines available to doctors to support them in their diagnosis of mental conditions.

The key symptoms of depression, as defined by these guidelines, are:

- persistent sadness or low mood
- loss of interest or pleasure in activities.

In order to be diagnosed with depression, you will be experiencing at least one of these two symptoms, most days and for most of the time, over a period of at least 2 weeks.

Additional symptoms may include:

- fatigue and low energy
- disturbed or excessive sleep
- low self-esteem
- altered appetite – specifically a change in body weight of at least 5% in 1 month
- feelings of guilt, worthlessness
- poor concentration, indecisiveness
- slowing of movements
- agitation
- loss of pleasurable feelings
- loss of sex drive
- suicidal thoughts or acts.

> The International Classification of Diseases (ICD-10) and the Diagnostic and Statistical Manual of Mental Disorders (DSM-IV) offer the most recognised criteria for depression.

Diagnostic tools

Your doctor may use a questionnaire to establish a diagnosis of depression. These vary in the number of questions they contain, but all are in a clear, multiple-choice format, and simply ask you for honest answers about your feelings. If you are asked to complete a questionnaire, just remember that there are no right or wrong answers – it is important that you don't try to bias your answers towards what you think they should be!

Depression is not diagnosed by a blood test or a scan, but purely on the basis of symptoms. However, don't be surprised if your doctor asks for a blood sample, as they will want to exclude other causes of your symptoms, before embarking on a treatment plan that is right for you.

Complicating the diagnosis

Despite its defining symptoms, depression is not an easy condition to diagnose. You may have physical aches and pains which can mask the emotional symptoms, and your depression may be overshadowed by other chronic conditions such as diabetes or heart disease.

Before embarking on any treatment, your doctor will want to exclude a number of other possible factors which may account for your persistent low mood. In these cases, treatment or eradication of these factors would be more appropriate than treatment for depression. These factors include:

- another medical condition (e.g. anaemia [low number of red blood cells in your blood] or hypothyroidism [an underactive thyroid], both of which cause symptoms which could be mistaken for those of depression)
- side-effects from the treatment of another medical condition
- abuse of drugs or alcohol.

Your doctor must also distinguish depression from the normal sadness that accompanies bereavement, for example. These deep feelings can persist for longer in some people than others, and can sometimes be confused with depression.

Around half of patients with depression who consult their GP will not be diagnosed at their first appointment.

TREATMENT GUIDELINES

There are two main aims when treating clinical depression.

■ To alleviate the current feelings of depression.

■ To reduce the risk of future episodes of depression.

The NICE guidelines place particular emphasis on the importance of your own preference when a doctor is choosing how to treat your depression.

There are a number of possible treatments available for these purposes, and it is the severity of your condition that determines which approach your doctor will take. Doctors in the UK can refer to nationally accepted guidelines for advice about how best to treat patients with depression. The most authoritative guidelines in the UK are published by the National Institute for Health and Clinical Excellence (NICE). This is a summary of the recommendations made by NICE for the treatment options available for each severity of depression.

Mild depression:

■ watchful waiting (with exercise plans and sleep/relaxation strategies)

■ antidepressant drugs are unlikely to be used at this stage

■ talking treatments (e.g. guided self-help, problem-solving therapy, cognitive behavioural therapy, counselling).

Moderate depression:

- antidepressant drugs
- talking treatments (e.g. cognitive behavioural therapy), but usually only if response to antidepressant drugs remains inadequate after a fair trial.

Severe depression:

- combination of antidepressant drugs and talking treatments from the outset
- antipsychotic drugs if experiencing delusions/hallucinations
- lithium
- electroconvulsive therapy (ECT) as an emergency treatment option.

Referral to a mental health specialist

You can expect to be referred to a mental health specialist if:
- your depression cannot be adequately controlled by your GP
- your GP considers you to be at significant risk of self-harm or suicide
- you are 'sectioned' under the Mental Health Act of 1983.

TREATMENT OPTIONS FOR DEPRESSION

The way in which your doctor decides to treat your depression depends on how serious it appears to be. The three main approaches are – **watchful waiting**, **talking treatments** and **antidepressant drugs**. There are also a number of less commonly used options.

WATCHFUL WAITING

'Watchful waiting' describes a period of time in which both you and your doctor will keep a close eye on your symptoms, taking note of any improvement or deterioration. There will be no treatment, either with drugs or psychological approaches, during this time.

It might be a good idea to keep a symptom diary during the watchful waiting period so that you can accurately report your symptoms and feelings to your doctor on your return visit.

If your doctor decides to take this approach, this does not mean that your symptoms are being dismissed or not taken seriously. Given that drug treatments for depression have side-effects, and psychological therapies are time-consuming, costly and not always available, it is in your best interests to avoid using these treatments if they are not necessary. You will normally be asked to return in 2 weeks or so, and it is important that you do so, as the doctor needs to assess whether the watchful waiting approach has been sufficient, or whether your treatment needs to be stepped up.

TALKING TREATMENTS

Counselling

This is the least structured of the psychological approaches. A counsellor will not give you advice, but will ask questions which will stimulate you to think about how to resolve your own difficulties. Counselling is based on the idea that sharing your problems helps you to take a fresh view and develop ideas for yourself on how to work through these problems. Typically, you might have one session a week, initially just for a few weeks, though this could be extended if the treatment is beneficial.

Different counsellors will have individual backgrounds and techniques, so you may need to try more than one before you find someone who really helps you. You should always aim to use a counsellor who is accredited with the British Association for Counselling and Psychotherapy (BACP; *www.bacp.co.uk*).

The Mental Health Act

If an approved social worker or a close relative requests for you to be detained in hospital for treatment, and their application receives sufficient support from medical professionals, you may be 'sectioned' under the Mental Health Act of 1983. This legislation from the government's Department of Health ensures that you are detained in hospital and treated accordingly, until the doctor is satisfied of your recovery or the section expires. For more information, see *www.dh.gov.uk*

Specific psychological therapies

These types of therapy are more structured and specific than counselling. They can only be offered by a trained therapist, and unfortunately, there are very few of these in the UK. As a result, there is only limited availability of specific psychological therapies on the NHS. It is common, for example, to wait over 6 months or even as much as a year for cognitive behavioural therapy on the NHS.

Cognitive behavioural therapy (CBT)

This aims to change abnormal patterns of behaviour. You may be asked to keep a diary of your symptoms, thoughts and behaviour, and your therapist will work with you to develop more positive ways of thinking and to dispel any false beliefs. Typically, a course of CBT would involve between six and eight sessions over a period of about 10 weeks.

Problem-solving therapy

This aims to identify the major problems in your life which may be contributing to your depression. Your therapist will work with you to generate practical and achievable solutions to these problems, which you will be asked to put into action between sessions. Typically, you would receive around six sessions over a period of 3 months.

Interpersonal therapy

This technique aims specifically to improve your social skills and the quality of your close relationships. Your spouse or partner may be asked to attend these sessions with you (in which case your treatment may be referred to as couple-focused therapy). Typically, sessions might be weekly for a period of 3 to 4 months.

Guided self-help

Due to the very limited availability of the specific psychological therapies on the NHS, guided self-help aims to offer similar types of therapy without the need for a trained therapist. This may be done by means of reading material (**bibliotherapy**) or interactive computer programmes (which are generally based on CBT). If you use guided self-help, you can work through the therapy at your own pace, but you should keep up regular contact, perhaps by phone, with a member of your care team, who will be able to monitor your progress.

Befriending

Your doctor can arrange for someone (usually a volunteer) to visit you for general friendly chats, and perhaps to accompany you on excursions. They will probably visit on a weekly basis, for several months. This can be very useful for people who are socially isolated. However, if you take part in a befriending scheme, it is important to recognise that you still need to make the effort to get out and actively make other friends, so that you don't become too dependent on your befriender.

KEEP IN REGULAR CONTACT WITH A MEMBER OF YOUR CARE TEAM.

ANTIDEPRESSANT DRUGS

We have already seen how the available antidepressant drugs work to restore neurotransmitter levels in the brain. Certain classes of antidepressants (such as selective serotonin reuptake inhibitors [SSRIs] and atypical drugs like venlafaxine) are considered preferable to others, not so much because they are significantly more effective, but more due to the lower risk of side-effects that have been shown with the more recently developed drugs.

The table opposite includes a full list of all the antidepressant drugs used by doctors for treating depression in the UK.

All of these drugs take between 2 and 3 weeks to start to work. At least 6 weeks of treatment, and often longer, is required for the full response to be achieved. Unfortunately, there is a reasonable chance that the drugs won't be effective at all. SSRIs, TCAs and MAOIs are all effective in roughly two-thirds to three-quarters of patients with depression.

Up to half of the benefits achieved with antidepressants may be due to the psychological impact of taking a pill.

Drug class	Generic name	Brand name
Selective serotonin reuptake inhibitors (SSRIs)	Citalopram	Cipramil®
	Escitalopram	Cipralex®
	Fluoxetine	Prozac®
	Fluvoxamine maleate	Faverin®
	Paroxetine	Seroxat®
	Sertraline	Lustral®
Monoamine oxidase inhibitors (MAOIs)	Phenelzine	Nardil®
	Isocarboxazid	Isocarboxazid
	Tranylcypromine	Tranylcypromine
	Moclobemide	Manerix®
Tricyclic antidepressants (TCAs)	Amitriptyline	Triptafen®, Triptafen-M®
	Amoxapine	Asendis®
	Clomipramine	Anafranil®, Anafranil SR®
	Doxepin	Sinequan®
	Imipramine	Tofranil®
	Lofepramine	Feprapax®, Lomont®, Gamanil®
	Nortryptyline	Allegron®, Motival®
	Trimipramine	Surmontil®
Atypical antidepressants	Flupentixol	Fluanxol®
	Mirtazapine	Zispin SolTab®
	Reboxetine	Edronax®
	Tryptophan	Optimax®
	Venlafaxine	Efexor®, Efexor® XL
	Maprotiline	Ludiomil®
	Mianserin	Mianserin
	Trazodone	Molipaxin®

Drugs often have more than one name. A generic name, which refers to its active ingredient, and a brand name, which is the trade name given to it by the pharmaceutical company. Fluoxetine is a generic name and Prozac® is a brand name.

Unfortunately, antidepressant drugs have side-effects, some of which can be particularly unpleasant or even dangerous. Your doctor will select your treatment carefully, making sure that you do not have any other medical conditions which are likely to make your antidepressant treatment dangerous. The doctor will also advise you on whether there are any foods you ought to avoid whilst being treated, and what side-effects to look out for.

MAOIs can cause unpleasant, and potentially dangerous, side-effects if taken in combination with certain foods, such as aged cheese, aged or cured meats and yeast extract.

The table opposite shows some of the most frequent side-effects of antidepressant drugs. Don't be alarmed by these lists – your doctor will be able to minimise your risk of developing side-effects by taking into account your medical background when choosing your drug.

If you experience symptoms which you think may be due to the medication you are taking, you should talk to your doctor or pharmacist. If the side-effect is unusual or particularly severe, your GP may decide to report it to the Medicines and Healthcare Products Regulatory Agency (MHRA).

Drug class	Typical side-effects
Selective serotonin reuptake inhibitors (SSRIs)	Gastrointestinal problems, dry mouth, nervousness, anxiety, headache, insomnia, tremor, dizziness, hallucinations, drowsiness, sexual dysfunction, urinary retention, sweating, visual disturbances.
Monoamine oxidase inhibitors (MAOIs)	Postural hypotension (low blood pressure when standing up causing fainting, dizziness), dizziness, drowsiness, insomnia, headache, dry mouth, gastrointestinal problems, oedema (fluid-filled swellings), agitation, tremors, arrhythmias (abnormal heart beat), sexual disturbances, confused state, nervousness, blurred vision, sweating, rashes, weight gain.
Tricyclic antidepressants (TCAs)	Effects on heart and blood vessels (e.g. postural hypotension, irregular/slow/fast heart beat), convulsions, drowsiness, blurred vision, constipation, urinary retention, sweating, tremor, headache, movement disorders, tinnitus (noise in the ear or head generated inside the body), fevers, abnormal sexual function.
Atypical antidepressants	Due to the number and variety of drugs in this collection, please refer to the patient information leaflet supplied with your medication or ask your doctor.

The MHRA operates a 'Yellow Card Scheme' which is designed to flag up potentially dangerous drug effects and thereby protect patient safety. The procedure has changed recently to allow patients to report adverse drug reactions themselves. Visit www.yellowcard.gov.uk for more information.

THE DRUG DEVELOPMENT PROCESS

Developing and launching a new drug onto the commercial market is an extremely costly and time-consuming venture. The process can take a pharmaceutical company between 10 and 15 years from the outset, at an estimated cost of £500 million. Much of this time is spent fulfilling strict guidelines set out by regulatory authorities in order to ensure the safety and quality of the end product. Once registered, a new drug is protected by a patent for 20 years, after which time other rival companies are free to manufacture and market identical drugs, called generics. Thus, the pharmaceutical company has a finite period of time before patent expiry to recoup the costs of drug development and return a profit to their shareholders.

During the development process, a drug undergoes five distinct phases of rigorous testing – the preclinical phase, which takes place in the laboratory – and phases 1, 2, 3 and 4, which involve testing in humans. Approval from the regulatory body and hence, a licence to sell the drug, is dependent on the satisfactory completion of all phases of testing. In the UK, the Medicines and Healthcare Products Regulatory Agency (MHRA) and the European Medicines Evaluation Agency (EMEA) regulate the drug development process.

- Only about 1 in every 100 drugs that enter the preclinical stage progress into human testing because they failed to work or have unacceptable side-effects.
- Animal testing is an important part of drug development. Before a drug reaches a human, it is vital that its basic safety has been established in an animal. Researchers do everything in their powers to minimise the number of animals they use and must adhere to strict guidelines issued by the Home Office.
- Phase 1 testing takes place in groups of 10–80 healthy volunteers.
- Phase 2 testing takes place in 100–300 patients diagnosed with the disease the drug is designed to treat.
- Phase 3 clinical trials involve between 1,000 and 3,000 patients with the relevant disease, and look at both the short- and long-term effects of the drug.
- Phase 4 testing and monitoring continues after the drug has reached the market.

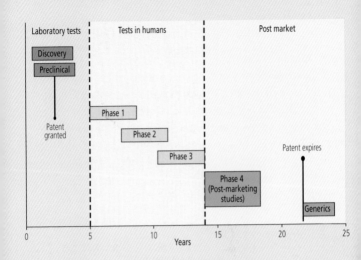

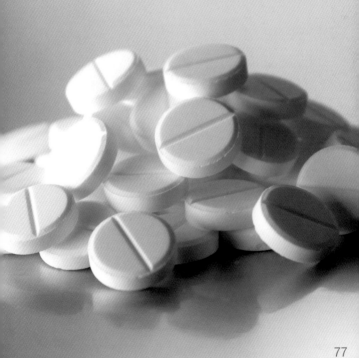

STOPPING ANTIDEPRESSANT TREATMENT

You may be surprised at how long you are advised to continue taking your antidepressant medication. If your depression is recurrent, this may be as long as several years. Remember that you have been given these drugs not only to relieve your current symptoms of depression, but also to minimise the risk of them coming back. It is this latter reason that makes it so important that you do take the drugs for as long as you are advised, even when you feel better and don't think that you need them any more.

> *Although in most cases, patients are advised to take their antidepressants for at least 6 months, it is estimated that only about half take them for any longer than 1 month.*

You may wish to stop your antidepressants because of the side-effects that they are causing. It may be useful to know that some side-effects are worse when you first start taking the drugs, and will lessen with time, so wherever possible it is best to persist with taking them.

If the drugs are not effective, or if the side-effects are proving too much for you, it is important that you tell your doctor, who will oversee you coming off the treatment gradually, over the course of about a month if possible. Stopping the treatment suddenly (or even missing doses or reducing the dose) can cause a phenomenon known as **discontinuation syndrome**. This is associated with unpleasant side-effects, such as nausea, vomiting, headaches, anxiety, dizziness, chills, insomnia and vivid dreaming. Certain antidepressants, such as paroxetine (Seroxat®) and venlafaxine (Efexor®, Efexor® XL) carry a particularly high risk of causing discontinuation syndrome.

Some people mistake discontinuation syndrome for a sign that antidepressants are addictive. This is not the case – if you are taking antidepressants, you don't need to keep increasing the dose in order for them to keep being effective, and you won't crave the drugs when you stop taking them.

Antidepressants and suicide

You may have heard stories in the media claiming that antidepressants, and particularly SSRIs, can increase your risk of suicidal thoughts and actions. Seroxat® (paroxetine) has been the focus of much of this attention. The data concerning the risk of suicide and self-harm whilst taking SSRIs have now been extensively reviewed by an independent body in the UK – the Committee on Safety of Medicines (CSM). By analysing clinical trial data, the CSM reported that an increased risk of suicide when treated with SSRIs compared with a placebo drug cannot be ruled out. They did not, however, identify any clear evidence that SSRIs were any more dangerous in this respect than other classes of antidepressant drugs.

All antidepressants cause side-effects and sometimes they can be very serious.

When deciding whether or not it is safe to prescribe a drug, the doctor has to weigh up the balance of risk and benefit. If the benefits outweigh the risk, then it may be worthwhile to take the drug, but there will inevitably be a small proportion of cases where the risks manifest themselves.

Consideration of the risk–benefit ratio has severely restricted the use of antidepressants in children. Fluoxetine (Prozac®) is the only SSRI which is considered, on the basis of clinical trial data, to have a favourable risk–benefit balance in patients under the age of 18. SSRIs are licensed for use in young adults, but as some people mature more quickly than others, a doctor will monitor young adults receiving SSRIs particularly closely.

WHAT TO DO IF YOU FEEL SUICIDAL

If you are having suicidal thoughts, and feel that you might put yourself, or indeed others, in danger, you need to get help immediately. Call an ambulance, and explain how you are feeling. Let someone close to you know what is happening, and try to get them to come and stay with you until help arrives or to take you to the nearest hospital.

If you don't feel that you are in immediate danger, but are having thoughts about suicide or self-harm, make sure that you tell your doctor at the next available opportunity. Your treatment may need to be stepped up and you may need support beyond that which your GP can provide during routine appointments.

OTHER TREATMENTS

St John's wort

St John's wort is a plant (full name *Hypericum perforatum*), extracts of which are available in the form of capsules, from chemists, supermarkets and health food shops. A number of different formulations of St John's wort are available, with varying potencies. It is not a licensed drug, and has not been through the same kind of rigorous testing for safety and effectiveness that drugs such as antidepressants have to by law.

St John's wort is generally considered to be fairly effective, at least in treating mild or moderate depression. It is thought that the antidepressant action may be similar to that of SSRIs (inhibition of the reuptake of serotonin into the pre-synaptic neuron). St John's wort also has a range of other effects, some of which, it appears, interact with the functioning of other drugs. It is known to reduce the effectiveness of the oral contraceptive pill, and also affects the activity of certain drugs used to treat:

- high cholesterol and heart disease
- migraine
- eczema
- HIV.

St John's wort may even affect the function of other antidepressant drugs. It is vital, therefore, that you tell your doctor if you are taking this supplement.

SOURCE: NATIONAL WILD FLOWER CENTRE.

Electroconvulsive therapy

Electroconvulsive therapy was originally used in the 1930s for treating schizophrenia.

If you are receiving care from a mental health specialist, electroconvulsive therapy (ECT) is available as a treatment option. For some patients, ECT can be an effective treatment.

ECT can seem a rather unpleasant procedure – doctors apply an electrical pulse, which lasts a few seconds, to the scalp. This causes a generalised, but controlled, brain fit (or seizure). The procedure is, however, carried out under a general anaesthetic which makes it less distressing for the patient. The process has been shown to improve neurotransmission by noradrenaline and dopamine, similar to the effects of treatment with antidepressant drugs. Although it is effective in the majority of cases, the benefits only tend to last for a few weeks. It is rarely used as a long-term treatment option, but can provide

important relief when depression is at its most severe.

ECT is considered to be no more dangerous that any other surgical operation which is carried out under general anaesthetic. Some patients may experience patchy memory loss, headaches and muscle aches. As yet, however, there is no evidence that ECT causes any long-term damage in the brain or widespread long-term memory problems.

You cannot be treated with ECT until you have given consent, providing that you are well enough to do so. You are free to withdraw this consent at any time. If you are not in a fit state to offer your consent (usually if you have been sectioned under the Mental Health Act), the decision over whether or not to treat you with ECT will be made by a second, independent doctor, who has not been involved in your treatment up until that point.

ECT acts much more quickly than other treatments, and induces a marked improvement in more than 9 out of 10 patients.

Mental health specialists may also use more experimental options if they consider them appropriate.

- **Deep brain stimulation** – electrodes are surgically implanted in regions of the brain thought to be involved in depression, and used to stimulate these regions with electricity.
- **Vagal nerve stimulation** – a tiny pacemaker-like device is inserted under the skin on the upper chest and an electrode is implanted in the neck. Together, these are used to electrically stimulate the vagal nerve, which connects with emotional centres in the brain.
- **Transcranial magnetic stimulation** – magnets are placed on the scalp for a short time to alter the electrical currents in the brain.
- **Neurosurgery.**

Other options

There are numerous alternative therapies which are thought by some to be beneficial in depression. These have not been rigorously tested in clinical studies, and so neither their effectiveness nor their safety can be guaranteed. These options include:

■ acupressure/acupuncture
■ Alexander technique (involves the redistribution of muscle tension)
■ aromatherapy
■ herbal medicine
■ homeopathy
■ hypnotherapy
■ imagery/visualisation
■ magnet therapy
■ massage
■ meditation
■ music therapy
■ reflexology
■ yoga.

EXERCISE AND DEPRESSION

Although doctors readily admit that antidepressants are not effective in all patients and can cause unpleasant side-effects, they are not left with many alternative options. There is at least a 6-month waiting list for talking treatments in some areas. There has recently been growing interest, however, in a cheap, effective therapy which has *positive* side-effects – exercise! Most people who take regular exercise will tell you that it puts them in a good mood, and few doctors would disagree with exercise being a good thing for someone who is depressed.

In one study of prescribing behaviour, over three-quarters of GPs claim to have prescribed antidepressants despite believing that an alternative approach would be preferable.

Regular exercise can actually be as effective as antidepressant drugs or talking treatments in relieving symptoms in mild cases of depression. There are a number of ways in which exercise could improve your mood:

- it increases your level of endorphins (proteins which act in a similar way to morphine, making you less sensitive to pain)
- it improves the way you look, and therefore your self-esteem
- it provides a social setting for meeting new people.

'Endorphin' literally means 'endogenous morphine'.

It is important to consult your doctor before engaging in any new kind of exercise. Certain forms of exercise may be unsuitable for you, given other conditions that you may have (e.g. osteoporosis). There are approximately 1,300 exercise referral schemes now active in the UK, whereby a GP can refer a patient to a fitness instructor. These are not widely used at present, but there is a lot of emphasis on your own personal preference when it comes to your doctor deciding how best to treat you, so if you are interested, ask if an exercise referral is available to you.

The number of antidepressants prescribed by GPs in the UK has more than doubled since the mid 1970s.

DIET AND DEPRESSION

Maintaining a healthy diet is particularly important if you suffer from depression. A loss of appetite is a common feature of the condition, and it is important to overcome this, because a lack of certain components from your diet can serve to make depression worse. There are a number of vitamins and fatty acids which are often found to be lacking in the diets of depressed people, and are recommended as dietary supplements for managing the condition.

Omega-3 fatty acids

Omega-3 fatty acids are a group of fatty substances which are found in polyunsaturated fats. They are important components of the membranes which surround the cells of our body, particularly neurons. The best source of omega-3 fatty acids is oily fish, such as mackerel or sardines. Clinical studies have demonstrated that depressed patients whose diets were supplemented with omega-3 fatty acids showed improvements above those they were already receiving through conventional therapy. If you are not keen on the taste of oily fish, you can buy fish oil supplements from health food shops, supermarkets and pharmacies.

Fatty acids make up 15% of the brain's weight, and deficiencies in these nutrients are thought to be involved in several mental health problems.

B vitamins

Three members of the vitamin B family are believed to be particularly beneficial for patients with depression: **vitamin B6**, **vitamin B9 (folic acid)** and **vitamin B12**. Vitamin B6 is thought to be especially useful for normalising hormone imbalances in women who are taking the contraceptive pill.

GOOD SOURCES OF B VITAMINS:

Vitamin B6	Vitamin B9 (folic acid)	Vitamin B12
Potatoes	Asparagus	Meat
Breakfast cereals	Peas	Dairy products
Meat, fish	Whole grains	Fish
Nuts and seeds	Nuts	Eggs
Eggs	Liver, kidney	Yeast extract
Bananas	Yeast	Seaweed

Tryptophan

Tryptophan is a naturally occurring amino acid (amino acids are the building blocks of proteins) which is used in the body to make serotonin. Some foods contain substantial amounts of tryptophan, and eating these is thought to boost your serotonin levels, and therefore may help to combat depression. Good sources of tryptophan include bananas, eggs, milk, cheese, yoghurt, oats, chicken and turkey.

Chocolate contains a fatty substance from the cannabinoid family. It mimics the effect of marijuana in the brain, which may explain why some people swear that chocolate boosts their mood!

DEPRESSION IN THE WORKPLACE

Around 20% of work absences in the UK are due to depression.

It is likely that issues at work may have contributed to your developing depression. Facing work can be one of the biggest hurdles in overcoming your condition.

You may be concerned about admitting to your employers that you are suffering from depression, for fear of discrimination. However, if you do decide to discuss your condition openly with your employer, they may be able to help. Your employer is required by law not to discriminate against mentally ill or disabled employees or job applicants (unless they employ fewer than 15 people or are exempt due to the nature of the work, e.g. emergency services, armed forces). This means that they must not favour other employees above you purely because of your condition, and they must make reasonable adjustments to accommodate you. The main body of legislation concerning unfair treatment in the workplace is the *Disability Discrimination Act 1995*. See the government's Disability Policy Division website for more details: *www.disability.gov.uk/dda*

If you are asked questions at a job interview about your mental health and previous time off work, you are legally obliged to tell your potential employer the truth.

There are steps that you can take yourself to make working with depression more bearable:

- take it easy – don't rush back to work too soon
- try to avoid long hours and unsociable night shifts
- plan activities outside work that you can look forward to
- over time, build up the challenges that you are prepared to tackle.
- make sure you get enough sleep.

Many people with depression (particularly men) try to hide or ignore it by working longer hours. It is important not to bury yourself in your work as a way to escape the outside world. Make sure you establish a good work–life balance.

Returning to work after a period of absence can actually help you to overcome your depression, as it provides:

- social contact
- structure to the day
- self-esteem.

POSTNATAL DEPRESSION

Postnatal depression affects around 1 in 10 mothers and 1 in 25 fathers.

Postnatal depression is more serious than the baby blues, which affects approximately half of new mothers in the UK. Usually occurring within the first 2 months after childbirth, postnatal depression can take the form of mild depression, or can become more severe and long term. The most severe form, **puerperal psychosis**, is much more rare. Most people assume that only mothers get postnatal depression. This is not true – fathers can experience it too.

The symptoms of postnatal depression are very similar to general depression. However, there may also be some symptoms specifically relating to the new baby, such as obsessive fears about the baby's health, or perhaps even thoughts of harming the child. The symptoms of puerperal psychosis usually begin as feelings of restlessness, excitement and insomnia. However, these might then be replaced by delusions, hallucinations, mania and dramatic mood swings.

What causes it?

Childbirth is a stressful experience for any mother, and is followed by a huge increase in responsibility and a loss of freedom. It is thought that a difficulty adapting to a lack of the hormone progesterone might be one of the reasons behind postnatal depression.

Any mother can get postnatal depression, though there are certain risk factors which make it more likely:

- a previous history of depression
- financial worries
- long periods being left alone with the new baby
- having relationship difficulties with the other parent
- physical problems after the birth, such as urinary incontinence.

Some of these risk factors also apply to a new father, who is also thought to be more likely to experience postnatal depression if the mother is depressed.

How is it treated?

Often, much of the problem in postnatal depression arises from feelings of isolation and a lack of support. Therefore, getting support and help from family and friends is usually a very effective step in overcoming postnatal depression. Other steps you can take yourself include:

- get out and meet other new mothers – try the Meet a Mum Association (MAMA) *www.mama.co.uk*
- look after yourself – make sure you eat properly and get regular breaks from being left to care for your baby on your own
- get plenty of exercise
- learn relaxation techniques.

It is important to get postnatal depression treated properly, as it can affect the emotional, behavioural and intellectual development of your child.

Along with practical support and advice, talking treatments can be very helpful in postnatal depression.

Your doctor may recommend that you take antidepressant drugs to overcome your condition. Many new mothers worry about the effects of taking these drugs whilst breast-feeding. It is true that a small amount of the drug will get into your breast milk, and so will be passed onto your baby. Experts believe, however, that the baby's body is perfectly capable of breaking down the drugs and so should not suffer any ill effects.

If you are concerned about taking antidepressants whilst breast feeding, speak to your doctor, who will be able to advise you.

If you are overly anxious, and having trouble sleeping, your doctor may prescribe you a tranquilliser, such as valium. If you have puerperal psychosis, you may be prescribed antipsychotic drugs and lithium to stabilise your mood, and doctors may recommend electroconvulsive therapy.

POSTNATAL DEPRESSION AFFECTS AROUND 1 IN 25 FATHERS.

SEASONAL AFFECTIVE DISORDER

In the UK, approximately 4% of the population are diagnosed with seasonal affective disorder and require treatment.

Seasonal affective disorder (sometimes abbreviated to SAD) is also known as 'winter depression'. It has most impact between the months of September and April, and particularly during the midwinter months, November to January. In most cases it is associated with fairly mild symptoms of depression, and often remains undiagnosed, but in more severe forms it can be seriously disabling.

The symptoms are very similar to depression, though with particular emphasis on sleep problems. People with seasonal affective disorder are often fatigued and tend to oversleep, although some suffer disturbed sleep. There is also a tendency to over-eat and put on weight.

What causes it?

It is not entirely clear what causes seasonal affective disorder, but it appears that daylight is the most important factor.

There is an interesting link between daylight and the level of serotonin in your brain, which, as you know, is involved in controlling mood and emotions. When it's dark, a tiny gland in your brain called the **pineal gland** produces a hormone called **melatonin**. Melatonin is involved in making you sleep when it is dark. The important thing here is that the pineal gland uses serotonin to make melatonin.

It appears that if you have seasonal affective disorder, your melatonin levels are abnormally high during the winter months. As serotonin is used to make melatonin, these seasonal increases in melatonin may impair serotonin function.

In the same way as depression, it is thought that stressful life experiences and hormonal upheavals are amongst the triggers for seasonal affective disorder.

How is it treated?

Your doctor may treat seasonal affective disorder with antidepressants in the same way as they would for any other kind of depression. However, often the first choice of treatment is light therapy (**phototherapy**). The theory behind this treatment is that it will reduce the rate at which your pineal gland tries to generate melatonin, thus increasing the amount of serotonin in your brain.

Phototherapy involves spending between 1 and 4 hours each day exposed to bright light (at least ten times brighter than an ordinary light bulb). It is important that you use a light box designed specifically for this purpose, in order to avoid exposure to dangerous levels of ultraviolet (UV) light (a sunbed, for example, is not suitable for this purpose).

You may experience some headaches or irritability whilst having a course of phototherapy, and it is important that you have your eyes checked regularly, but the side-effects are generally mild and rare compared with those you might experience with antidepressants. Once your treatment is well established, and if it is working effectively, you may not need to use the light source every day. It is a good idea to involve

Phototherapy is effective in approximately 4 out of 5 people.

For ideas on light boxes, try *www.sadbox.com* or *www.outsidein.co.uk*

your doctor in this treatment from the outset, so that you have a professional source of advice and any other treatment you are receiving can be tailored accordingly.

There are a number of other things you can do to help yourself overcome seasonal affective disorder. As well as the general advice for depression, such as getting plenty of exercise and eating well, try to:

- spend as much time outdoors as possible, and sit near a window when you are indoors
- simplify your life in winter – put off any life-changing decisions until spring!

SPECIAL PATIENT POPULATIONS

Children

Depression is less common in children than in adults, but many people are not aware that it can occur in children at all. It is particularly difficult to recognise in young people, as tearfulness, irritability, altered sleep patterns and feelings of being left out or different are all, to a certain extent, normal in children and adolescents.

After the age of 8, the symptoms of depression in children are very similar to those in adults, but children with depression often come across as being 'stroppy' and difficult, rather than particularly sad. Of course, all children change their behaviour and sociability as they get older. However, if the mood is persistently low, it is worth asking a GP for advice, particularly if the child has a preoccupation with death or illness. Depression is particularly common in adolescent girls, and is often associated with eating disorders.

In childhood depression, the most important thing to look out for is a persistent change in mood.

The talking treatments which are available for use in adults can also be used for children, but hardly any antidepressants are recommended for use in the under 18s. The UK's Committee on Safety of Medicines (CSM) has advised that fluoxetine (Prozac®) is the only SSRI which can be used in children and adolescents. The emphasis, therefore, is on talking treatments for children with depression, with education of both the child and their family considered very important. The child's school can also provide support, in the form of a school counsellor, and general awareness of the child's condition.

The younger you are when you first develop depression, the more likely it is to recur.

During pregnancy

As you have seen, postnatal depression is a relatively common phenomenon, affecting both men and women after the birth of a child. However, women may also be affected during their pregnancy – roughly 1 in 10 women are reported to suffer from symptoms of depression half way through their pregnancy, and this figure rises for women in later stages of gestation.

Hormonal changes, as well as the stress of an imminent major life change, are probably factors involved in 'antenatal' depression. Many of the problems that can contribute to postnatal depression also apply at this earlier stage – strain on the relationship with the baby's father, financial concerns and less freedom to do previously enjoyable activities, for example.

There is no significant evidence to show that a mother's depression during pregnancy will have any noticeable effect on the baby once it is born, and worrying about this possibility will only serve to make the depression worse! Although it is best to minimise the use of drugs during pregnancy, you can take antidepressants whilst pregnant if talking treatments and other strategies are not effective. In many cases, depression which has been experienced during pregnancy will resolve spontaneously once the baby is born.

Elderly patients

Some people consider that mild depression is an inevitable part of growing old, and this can lead to cases of depression being easily missed in older patients. The most common age for depression to first occur is in the late 20s, but elderly people can develop depression, particularly if they have long-term medical complaints such as arthritis or back pain. Talking treatments are effective in elderly patients, but antidepressants are generally used more cautiously and often in lower doses due to their side-effects.

Although the majority of cases of depression in elderly people are mild, amongst men, the over-85 age group has the highest risk of suicide.

THE LONG AND SHORT OF IT

There is no denying that depression is a distressing condition, both for you and for your loved ones, who might be unsure of how best to help. First, you need to recognise that there is a problem and ask for help. If you are diagnosed with depression, remember that there is no quick fix. If your GP can treat you without the need for drugs, this is in your best interests, so keep an open mind to alternative approaches. If you are prescribed antidepressants, be aware of the time you need to allow for them to take effect and the dangers of coming off them too quickly.

Depression may go away if you leave it untreated, but there is a high risk that it will return. It is important to have it treated effectively, not only to speed up the improvement of your current symptoms, but also to minimise your risk of suffering episodes of depression in the future.

GETTING THE MOST OUT OF YOUR HEALTH SERVICE

Remember that there is no quick fix for depression. You and your doctor need to build a relationship which enables you to deal with the condition together, and work towards a long-term solution. If your doctor asks you to attend a follow-up appointment, it is very important that you do so. If you are not comfortable speaking to your doctor, perhaps it might be better to ask to see an alternative GP, as it is important that you can be open and frank about your symptoms, without feeling embarrassed or ashamed.

FIVE IDEAS FOR GETTING THE MOST OUT OF AN APPOINTMENT WITH YOUR GP

1 Send your GP a letter ahead of your appointment to explain your feelings and symptoms.

2 Take someone you trust to the appointment with you for moral support.

3 Write down your feelings before you attend the appointment. You could keep a diary to record your thoughts at the time you feel them.

4 Always attend your follow-up appointments.

5 Make sure you trust and get on with your GP. If not, ask to see a different doctor.

Having a doctor's appointment can be a daunting prospect. You probably have queries and concerns before you go into the surgery that completely fly out of your head when you are sat in front of the doctor! As well as making a written record of your symptoms and feelings before you go to your appointment, it may also help to write down a list of questions.

QUESTIONS TO ASK YOUR DOCTOR

- Will I receive drugs straight away?
- How do I get access to talking treatments?
- What is the waiting list like for talking treatments in this area?
- What side-effects should I expect from this particular drug?
- How should I involve my family? How much do they need to know?
- Do I need to tell my employer?
- Will my depression go away?
- Can I take St John's wort with the other treatments I am using?
- I am planning a pregnancy. Should I make any special preparations?
- What should I do if I start feeling suicidal?
- When should I come back for a follow-up appointment?

FURTHER READING

The Mental Health Foundation's 'Up and Running?' campaign
www.mentalhealth.org.uk/html/content/up_and_running.pdf

USEFUL CONTACTS:

■ **Association for Postnatal Illness**
Tel: 020 7386 0868
Website: *www.apni.org*

■ **Aware**
Support group for depression sufferers and their carers in
Northern Ireland
Tel: 02871 260602
Website: *www.aware-ni.org*

■ **Depression Alliance**
Tel: 020 7386 0868
Website: *www.depressionalliance.co.uk*

■ **Meet a Mum Association (MAMA)**
Provides contact with other mothers for friendship and
support.
Tel: 020 8768 0123 (7–10pm weekdays)
Website: *www.mama.co.uk*

■ **Mental Health Foundation**
Website: *www.mentalhealth.org.uk*

■ **Mind (National Association for Mental Health)**
Tel: 08457 660 163
Website: *www.mind.org.uk*

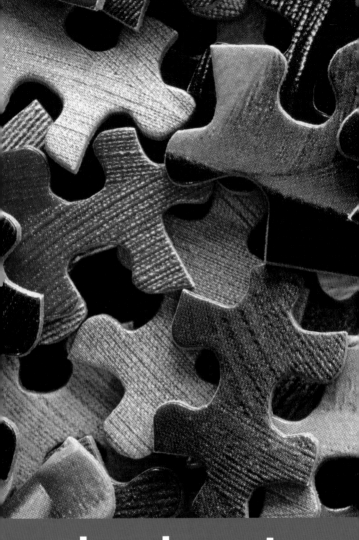

simple extras

■ **National Institute for Health and Clinical Excellence (NICE)**
11 The Strand
London
WC2N 5HR
Tel: 020 7766 9191
Website: *www.nice.org.uk*

■ **National Light Hire Company**
Website: *www.sadbox.com*

■ **NHS Direct**
NHS Direct Line: 0845 4647
Website: *www.nhsdirect.nhs.uk*

■ **The Patients Association**
PO Box 935
Harrow
Middlesex
HA1 3YJ
Tel: 020 8423 9111
Helpline: 08456 08 4455
Website: *www.patients-association.com*

■ **Royal College of Psychiatrists**
Website: *www.rcpsych.ac.uk*

■ **Samaritans**
Helpline: 08457 90 90 90
Email: *jo@samaritans.org*
Website: *www.samaritans.org*

■ **Saneline**
Out of hours telephone helpline for sufferers, carers and concerned relatives and friends.
Tel: 0845 767 8000

YOUR RIGHTS

As a patient, you have a number of important rights. These include the right to the best possible standard of care, the right to information, the right to dignity and respect, the right to confidentiality and underpinning all of these, the right to good health.

Occasionally, you may feel as though your rights have been compromised, or you may be unsure of where you stand when it comes to qualifying for certain treatments or services. In these instances, there are a number of organisations you can turn to for help and advice. Remember that lodging a complaint against your health service should not compromise the quality of care you receive, either now or in the future.

■ **Patients Association**
The Patients Association (*www.patients-association.com*) is a UK charity which represents patient rights, influences health policy and campaigns for better patient care.
Contact details:
PO Box 935
Harrow
Middlesex
HA1 3YJ
Helpline: 08456 084455
Email: *mailbox@patients-association.com*

■ **Citizens Advice Bureau**
The Citizens Advice Bureau (*www.nacab.org.uk*) provides free, independent and confidential advice to NHS patients at a number of outreach centres located throughout the country (*www.adviceguide.org.uk*).
Contact details:
Find your local Citizens Advice Bureau using the search tool at *www.citizensadvice.org.uk*

- **Patient Advice and Liaison Services (PALS)**
  Set up by the Department of Health (*www.dh.gov.uk*), PALS
  provide information, support and confidential advice to patients,
  families and their carers.
  Contact details:
  Phone your local hospital, clinic, GP surgery or health centre and
  ask for details of the PALS, or call NHS Direct on 0845 46 47.

- **The Independent Complaints Advocacy Service (ICAS)**
  ICAS is an independent service that can help you bring about
  formal complaints against your NHS practitioner. ICAS provides
  support, help, advice and advocacy from experienced advisors
  and caseworkers.
  Contact details:
  ICAS Central Team
  Myddelton House
  115–123 Pentonville Road
  London N1 9LZ
  Email: *icascentralteam@citizensadvice.org.uk*
  Or contact your local ICAS office direct.

Accessing your medical records

You have a legal right to see all your health records under the Data
Protection Act of 1998. You can usually make an informal request to
your doctor and you should be given access within 40 days. Note
that you may have to pay a small fee for the privilege.

You can be denied access to your records if your doctor believes
that the information contained within them could cause serious
harm to you or another person. If you are applying for access on
behalf of someone else, then you will not be granted access to
information which the patient gave to his or her doctor on the
understanding that it would remain confidential.

NOTES